BAY WINDOWS

The Land-The Sea-Beyond

BAY WINDOWS

The Land   -   The Sea   -   Beyond

Poems by
Leo Thibault

Bass River Press

South Yarmouth, Massachusetts

BASS RIVER PRESS

Printed by Lightning Source, Inc.
Edited by Angela Howes
Interior Design and Composition by Angela Howes
Cover art by Judith Brandon

Published by Bass River Press
307 Old Main St.
South Yarmouth, MA 02664
www.cultural-center.org

An imprint of the Cultural Center of Cape Cod, Bass River Press was
launched in 2014 to support literary artists from the Cape & Islands – and
has since devoted itself to publishing one book of poetry per year.
Poet Cleopatra Mathis judged the 2018 poetry competition and selected
Leo Thibault's manuscript for publication.

Library of Congress Control Number: 2019936239

Bass River Press is grateful for the support of the South Yarmouth Library
Association's Siemen Fund.

CULTURAL
CENTER
OF CAPE COD

All the Arts for All of Us

for Debra

flowers fade, friendship lasts

Acknowledgments

Thank you to the following publications in which these poems appeared, sometimes in earlier versions or with different titles:

PRINT

PHOTOGRAPH	Selections from First Night Chatham, 1998
DOG DAYS	Selections from First Night Chatham, 2001
BAGHDAD POINSETTIA	Poetry of Peace, April 2001
ESTATE SALE	Selections from First Night Chatham, 2002
EXTRAORDINARY RENDITION	Poetry of Peace, April 2006
JAMMING	Prime Time, April 2009
THE SILENT ONE	Prime Time, April 2015
FOUR BOYS ON A BEACH	Poetry of Peace, April 2015

ONLINE

ODE TO SPANISH MOSS	PEGallery.org, April 2011
BP AND ME	Pascoarts.org, April 2012
ONE MAN'S FRUIT STAND	Pascoarts.org, April 2012
BEACH GLASS	PEGallery.org, April 2013
THE HIVE	Pascoarts.org, April 2013
WAITING FOR AL AT THE NURSING HOME	Pascoarts.org, April 2017
VINCENT	Pascoarts.org, April 2017

CONTENTS

The Land

The Sea

Beyond

NOTES

The Land

JAMMING

It begins quietly:

the soft blue music of the bay
as a stage,

the tangled brush in the dunes,
stiff as strings, drawing blood from bare legs,

sprouting rainbow sounds:
yellow, blue, red

begging to be plucked, to drum
loudly into the metal bucket.

Later, in the kitchen

heat turned up, favorite colors
amplifying to a rollicking boil

it all jells together
in a syncopated carmine session

splattering beach plum notes
on the floor, the wall, the ceiling

creating a crimson crime scene
worthy of Miles Davis and Julia Child.

CHILDHOOD BLUES

" ... Restored to the mornings of childhood
When a drop of dew and a shout on the mountains
*Were the truth of the world." (*Czeslaw Milosz, *The Master)*

When I was a summery nine, I played
morning tennis with broken strings,
a cracked frame and bald grey spheres
on a pot-holed court, whacking away
merrily on the grimy red clay
exulting in the results.

Afternoons, I ran
through waist-high hayfields
bare legs rejoicing, still
unaware of a place called Lyme.
Shy, reluctant door-to-door peddler
of nature's exquisite, blue fruit,

when I reached the tangled patch
I stuffed fistfuls into my mouth
juices staining young cheeks,
old shirt, then plowed recklessly
through the dangerous ivy
to harvest the tastiest remains.

Later, speeding through town
pedaling a wild ride
on my trusted Schwinn,
unburdened of the blue gold, bucket
swinging from the handlebars
silver now rattling inside,

young, fearless capitalist, I owned
the world of creamy vanilla frappes
waiting to be poured
at Cleary's Drug Store
next to sweatshop mill no. 4
on the evening side of town.

OCTOBER IN THE PUNKHORN PARKLANDS

The ruffed grouse explodes
from the brush as I invade

his woods, rivers of autumn
streaming beneath my feet,

mushrooms jockeying for space
in a rainbow carpet where a few

green leaves struggle to survive.
After I leave, the oven-bird

stops complaining, the doe lowers
her white flag, turns to stare

and when the rotted pine falls,
the chipmunk squeals and scurries

through the noisy colors
into his dark home.

WAITING FOR AL AT THE NURSING HOME

A carpeted lobby, chandeliered and upholstered
for passing through, welcomes visitors.
Loveseats, hungry for occupation,
bracket the round glass-topped table
crowned by a glass chimney
protecting a candle that will never burn.

On an empty chest of drawers
a wooden goose looks heavenward
wishing it could take off
from its alien runway
and lose its plaid neckband.

Plastic ficus droops in opposite corners.
Generic pink and blue flowers
stretch the wallpaper all around,
reaching the white mantel where
bogus bittersweet attempts to crawl.

Al re-appears, his 95 years short-stepping
quickly through the pseudo-oriental
past the heavily-weighted grandfather's clock
ticking away.

He's visited his missus.
His smile beckons me to follow
past the exit sign
out into the sunlight.

BESTIARY

Sometimes,
I feel
like the carpenter ant facing
the bootsoles of apathy.

Other times,
I think
like the cockroach sitting
at the top of the evolutionary chain
who has trained me to feed him
my unswept crumbs.

More often,
I wonder
like the snapping turtle
neck on the line
whether I'll beat the 18-wheeler
across the highway divide.

Rarely, do I
dare imagine
the savannah lion
protecting the gazelle,
too sure
it will never happen.

ILLUSIONS

Whether he leans on air, mutely
plucks a coin from a surprised ear
or channels a rabbit
out of a top hat

we ache to believe
stake our lives on it.

But when he saws the coffin
in half, and his lovely
barely-clad accomplice
waves disjointed limbs at us

we nervously applaud
the surface of things.

THE SILENT ONE

He rarely spoke
while in his rocking chair,
content to back-and-forth
blowing wisps of smoke
from the slender pipe
clenched lightly between
stained and random teeth

or when trudging up the hill
from the sweatshop mill
empty lunchbox swaying,
every day of the 50 years
when machines blasted eardrums
and the heat sapped dreams

or quietly kneeling in the dirt
coaxing all the vegetables
to rise towards the dinner table,
angered only by woodchucks
and the snakes he used to fear

and attack with a frenzied,
very successful hoe
banishing their imagined sins
from his beloved garden

or the times he kissed his son
thinking he was asleep
and wouldn't notice.

BUS STOP

Alone

in the rain
leaning on the street sign

hands
turtled back
into Hilfiger sleeves

Air Nikes
peeking from
oversize Bauers

this child, this morning
stylishly backpacking wisdom
wears a sad, branded face

oblivious of the generic
blue-slickered mother standing by
an idling Grand Cherokee

Starbucks steam
and cold breath
mixing with the toxic fumes

that rise
and seemingly disappear,
like the child's body

waiting to be rescued
by the big yellow taxi

with the flashing red lights.

AIMEZ-VOUS **BALDWIN?**

Bien sur, je t'aime. How could I not ... ?
An elegant upright (with bench) precisely
abandoned in the Bell's Neck Conservation Area
of Harwich, waiting for ...

Chopin, Horowitz, Elton John
still mourning Diana, Victor Borge's jokes,
Liberace's sequined smile, perhaps
Condi Rice's imperial swan song?

Will raccoons plod nightly dissonance, snakes
slither across sharps *andante,* ospreys
perch stoically on flats, skunks
pump pedals *con brio*, squirrels
drop musical acorns, up-tailed chipmunks
scurry downscale *allegrissimo*?

Will songbirds scorn,
knowing superior music, except
for the mockingbird, flitting up and down
the abandoned ivories, enlarging his repertoire?

Who will play at night under the stars
when the keys are slippery wet?
Who will sit on the broiling August bench
when the audience is at the beach?

Will the lonely piano take root
branch out tall, burrow deep
back towards its beginning?

LOVE ON THE BEATEN EARTH

The fuzzy yellow sphere whistles by,
a spinning world to be struck
with gladiator determination
adroitly enough
to elude the Goliath opposite,
thinking same,

to be slammed, volleyed or finally
lobbed in desperation
into a gentle devastating arc
just beyond the Titan at the net.

Love?
Round as the zero it mimics
joyful as the ball in play
full as the universe at hand.

The cranberry clay creeps up
into virgin socks,
the net divides, disrupts
smothers every courtesy:
serve, return of serve,
advantage, let.

The ballet on the *terre battue* continues
until the multiplication of mindless faults
beyond assigned squares adds up to *nada* —
a love that is nothing
but a disservice
to one of the racquet-bearers.

In the end
they struggle to the net,
red dust now knee-high,
reach across
join tired hands, grateful
for this still irresistible dance.

A LITTLE KINDLING

Shyly he stumbles
towards my campsite
tripping twice
two-year-old arms extended
waving a bent twig
an offering to burn

then, eyes down
runs back to his mother's smile
and I am left holding
the beginnings of fire.

ESTATE SALE

In Brewster, Wellfleet, Bourne, they are announced
each one sad and beckoning, the end of an era or a life
changed forever by the classifieds,
to be sold for minor profit to strangers
surrendering to the allure of things.

Watch them now as they enter
tramping grey snow onto the faded Oriental
covering the undulating pine floor
underneath the massive sideboard
hugging the wall, priced to sell.

In the bathroom, remedies reveal infirmities
in the bedroom, desires hang discreetly in the closet
in the study, variegated minds line the bookshelves
in the kitchen, ingredients of meals never cooked, simmer
in the living room, once priceless curios, tacky/artful, preen.

To own is to pretend.

The seller has chosen, or suffered, a new direction.
Why should the milling crowd hunger
to recycle the past? The discarded desires,
the desiccated fronds of a life
sink into deceptive quicksand.

To disappear with grace, that is the art.

MINUET ON EGGSHELLS

They are the modern duo
of a kind
afraid to say
"you mean to me"
and all that follows.

Like two buzz saws slowly approaching
like two jousting knights bearing down
the teeth will fly
the knights will fall
but that's what happens

when two are all
they ever hoped for.

PHOTOGRAPH

A thousand times
I saw you reading
but never like this

capturing the lamp's light
that shapes your body
your fingers poised

to turn the pages
your heart devours
your forehead lined

with the pain of those
whose lives burst forth
from another's brain,

your cheek stained
by the overflow.
I could close my eyes

to remember you
or simply blink.

IN VINO VERITAS

If I never
see the night breeze
hear O'Keeffe's flowers
smell smooth velvet
touch Thanksgiving gravy
taste clay shapes

how will I ever
know a wine cantata
coursing down
the ruby throats
of ancient books
chorusing:

"swallow me ...
dim your pixilated screens,
sit down
at the splendid table
for a feast?"

HOME ...

an inner branch

                    where the robin stills
                    its flight at night

sings to the sun at dawn

a muddy hole

                    where the fiddler crab
                    sidles at low tide

to hide and survive

a cardboard carton

                    roofing a homeless grate,
                    or a comfortable home

cradling us, the restless

              who speed daily on miles of asphalt
              captive behind tinted windows

              or race cross-country on bullet trains
              shaking ancient railbeds

              or skystreak to foreign adventures
              pressurized, on slick wings

heading for a terminal

                    that never is — home,
                    embedded in the brain

as we round-trip back

                    to the warmth of the bed
                    in the empty room of the familiar,

the rest area

                    where, it seems,
                    we've seldom really lived.

DIVORCE

What if he had
come to believe
what she believed
about their cat, the way
he used to lie for hours
next to the chipmunk hole
in their front yard,
patient as a cheetah
trying to make a meal,
sometimes succeeding

or that both of them
could sit for a while
on the edge of the lawn
in those rickety Adirondacks
and talk about
the threads of the past
unraveling down
their own black hole,
could it not have lasted,
that meteor of trust
which illuminated
their night sky
in the beginning?

NOVEMBER

The wind chimes sing.
   The lone scrub pine
   collared by frosty impatiens and dyed-red chips
   bends, aging limbs protesting loudly.

The nimble squirrel swings
   on the thistle feeder, the sand flies
   on the strong north wind
   stings the coyote's face.

Under the floodlight
   by the pond
   he's already digesting
   a very convenient meal.

The washashore
   ensconced in his recliner
   by the window
   locks eyes with the wild brief presence

then quickly turns away
   calls twice for tabby
   clicks the remote
   searching for Survivors.

SWAN SONG

On the early morning water
necks questioning
arching into hearts
breasts forward,
they glide together smoothly
towards the rising heat,

so close, feathers velcroed,
offspring tethered behind
on a water-string
only they can see
and feel
and follow.

The barefoot couple
on the breakfast beach
hands cupping hips
walk in tandem
leaving recent ashes
to sear the cool sand.

Curved necks arcing,
darting
beneath the surface
they take turns to feed
and watch
over young ones
nestled in down
on the shore
of their backs,

sleeping,
unknowing
of the muskrat,
he too attracted
by the sky's heat,
sleek wet fur
skimming slowly
searching for
a dawn meal.

That evening
at dinner,
his neck
pulses with excitement
as she leans forward,
hearts united
fingers connected
to the embers within.

Later, after moonrise
post cappuccino
in the quiet colors
of the room above,
free from promises
they glide together
towards yet another
morning's fire.

The swans sleep,
fiery bills buried back
into wing down,
gently tossed
by their water hammock,
with each wave
touching each other
for life.

19

WHITE CAT, PARKED CAR

Ensconced full-length
against the rear window
of a Ford Focus, you do not need
our technological caveat:
objects in window
are closer than they appear.
Never looking back, you telescope
your vision to the hunger at hand.

Unknowing of your white beauty
you capture the proffered hand,
rub every digit, every circumference,
wrap yourself around
contorting beyond possibility,
tail drumming satisfaction.

When the strange hand, arrested
by the partially-closed window
can only quarter-turn awkwardly
to caress your furry snowstorm
and retreat, you distort your face
against the windshield in protest.

Then, you stretch and roll
in your hothouse world, ignoring
its confines and your inability
to leap out and dash madly
halfway up the nearest scrub pine
shredding the bark along the way
stopping suddenly
to question your wild desire.

VINCENT

Without his melancholy madness
we'd have plastic flowers
on collapsible card tables
and safe marigolds

in chalk-gray vases.
The lines of the mind
are far from straight,
they swirl and turn

and curve like Vincent's,
alive with vibrant shades
and heavy movements.
And who's to say

if they'll lead to churches
or solitary rooms?
Only the artist
whose agony gives them life

while giving up his own.
Vincent's chair cost him dearly,
the ones who see
we often label crazy.

There came a time
when Vincent couldn't stand
the screaming colors.
He sacrificed an ear

and with the other heard more
than all his friends combined.
Theo ran out of money
Vincent ran out of mind.
But while it lasted,
the two created
a bright yellow vision
that blinds.

KOYAANISQATSI
(*Life Out of Balance:* Hopi)

The cat can walk atop the picket fence.

But who will save us
from the top of the seesaw
the icy mountain ledge
the sagging tightrope?

Our teetering minds
explode with information
discover holes
in the world we revere

pain in the lives
and loves we share
hunger everywhere
blood in our laughter.

Our lives are out of balance
come and gone
quick as a mushroom
after a long summer rain.

The cat can walk
atop the picket fence
and sometimes slip
but never fall.

ODE TO SPANISH MOSS

Swaying with the wind
your tresses decorate the South.
Medusa of live oaks
you grace their branches
with welcoming leis
restoring some life
to these drab, desiccated trees.

Yet, your beauty is brittle,
breaks between my fingers
shattering illusions of elegance.
Perhaps that's why
we used to hide you
in mattresses, behind walls,
in the garden mulch.

But you, wedded to bark,
prefer to drink the rain,
feed on air, slowly inhale the breath
and mist around you, suck them in,
until they shape your rebel hair
that dances wildly the tango
that seduces me.

MEMOIR

He remembers older faces
frowning on his young attempts
to frolic, wander in the woods,
choose a career — no need now

to focus his pen like a laser
on their commandments, long
evaporated like the fantasies
they proudly dreamed for him.

He resists remembering in print,
refuses to cling to past
repeated "Nos," burden his days
with reconstructed tales

carry forward embellished
stories with weeping ink
explain failures
by mining the past

his archeology warping
into fantasy or fiction. Deeds
will justify his brief existence
on the planet.

He has let go
long ago. He is not —
can never be — what he was —
or someone thought he was.

No longer can anyone
create him. Every day now
the mirror in the hallway
reflects him.

The Sea

HIGH TIDINGS

The beach showers twice
      each day
            on schedule

receives the murky sea's
      smelly dandruff
            haphazardly

lines it up
      for the gulls
            to cull

and for the two-legged
      fitness stroller
            to examine intently

should he choose
      to find the time
            to connect

with the rest of the universe.

OYSTER SEASON

1.   Cleansed by thousands of tides
it clings to the safety of rock
hidden under the seagrass hair
unaware of the oysterman
who will pry it from its haven
slip it into a mesh bag
where it settles with its kin
tightly closed, resisting.

2.   The knife probes the razor edge
of the irregular shell
for the life-and-death spot
in the hinged entrance,
with a twist of the wrist
skill slips in, pops it open,
half-shell flies onto the trash pile,
exposing the floating flesh.

3.   The diner is served
this naked appetizer,
quivering in its briny pool
on a bed of ice
and he tilts it into his mouth
where eager lips surround
the throbbing, satin morsel,
search for the elusive pearl.

BEACH GLASS

I like to imagine your narrative
        as a fisherman's beer bottle,
                an Andrea Doria wine glass
                        perhaps an Outermost House windowpane

surrendered to the waves
        for decades of cleansing, polished by sand,
                etched by rocky bottoms
                        awakening at your passage the winter flounder

to end here at the wrack line
        with this soft sheen
                that invites stroking, dulled edges
                        no longer able to draw blood

tiny fragment of what was,
        carried back by admiring hands
                to a place of honor
                        on the fireplace mantel

given a second chance to shine.

RESURRECTION

I have left simple instructions:

to be flash-burned
white-hot, on deck,

then slowly sizzled into the sea

to be nibbled,
lukewarm by krill

and descend, cooling now

among the sleek dogfish
to finally settle,

scattered perhaps

on the cold, putrid bottom
of a lobster trap,

waiting to be devoured, and turn green

inside that hard black body
soon to rise again

be cracked open

and torn into shreds
at a gracious table,

but not before someone

feeding in celebration
has caused me to bleed again

all over my body.

WHEN THE NATIVES DISCOVERED COLUMBUS

You had to be there. When the Discoverer washed ashore
there were natives, skin dark, pride tall, already waiting,
not knowing the diseases and killings that were in store.

Bare torsos faced steel shells and Toledan swords galore,
and wondered what the cloud-pale faces were bringing
to them and their families as the Discoverer plodded ashore.

They approached each other, tentative and unsure
Columbus swaggering bravery — keen, native eyes exploring,
not seeing the smallpox and killings that were in store.

The "Indians" saw his bodyguards, the breastplates they wore
everything about them seemed warlike and menacing,
you had to be there when the Discoverer stumbled ashore.

Despite misgivings, the gentle people who were there before
gestured peace, bet on the white man's trivial offerings,
bad gamble: rape, slavery and killings still lay in store.

Now we have Columbus Day, a foliage weekend to tour,
a version of history authored by presidents and kings
who were not there when the Conquistador washed ashore,
who would oversee diseases and decimations by the score.

DOG DAYS

The watery wasteland
at Crosby Landing

dresses for January:
a bay without sails

without common eider
crunching mussels,

heaves its white flanks
on a desert of gray ice

its surging claws uncover
burrowed quahogs,

grind up the breakwater
piling icy rocks onshore.

A solitary chocolate lab
skates and slips in the distance

barks along the bay's
bright, icy spine

hyphenates the frozen sea
and its gently undulating shroud

denies it the permanence
it seems to crave.

SAINT'S LANDING

One summer morning,
after NPR delivered its daily dose
of current events,
a high tide of despair washed over
whatever flotsam of hope remained.

So he trudged half a mile out
off Saint's Landing, just east of Paine's Creek,
where his bare, searching toes
detected a sea clam, hard shell
nesting in soft sand.

And he bent,
and his hand
gently cupped one pound
of the sweetest bounty
dead low tide can offer.

No fear here in the ebbing eddies
circling his feet, just the wondrous
architecture and truth of a quiet life
trusting the advances
of a harvesting hand.

WATER LIVES

1.   The Diver

poised, toes gripping edge
blond hair capped,
leaps, jackknifes sleekly
into a straight clean plunge
carves out a small scoop
of the pool, sweeps up
to breathe with admiration
the perfection of her art.

2.   The Surfer

crouched, chutes the tunnel
curling wave cocooning
his amber Grecian body,
jelled hair undisturbed
skims the surface under the canopy
defies immersion, rides
the endless wave
of a chosen life.

3.   The Lifeguards

seated, greased, sun-glassed,
scan the whitecaps
hear the children at water's edge
screaming small discoveries,
observe the beached adults
reading blockbusters, baking pores,
dozing, know their relaxed muscles
could be summoned anytime
to dash, torpedo dragging
into the riptides.

SCRATCHING FOR LITTLENECKS

Sometimes a symphony happens
far away from cavernous halls
with their perfect acoustics
echoing the classics to an audience
knowing the outcome.

On opening day
movements of rakes on stone merge
to fill the air at Ellis Landing
with their low-tide composition.

As I approach the "rock pile"
dozens of players already there
fiddle steel tines that grow
into a dissonant, Cage-like overture.

Gulls enter off-beat punctuating the air;
the scratchers, without a conductor,
hunched over their instruments, complain
about the difficulty of the finale.

Garden hoes and waders,
rusted clam rakes and bare legs merge
to produce this one-week season
of a random orchestra
serenading the tidal flats.

MINDFULNESS

We sit at the edge of our sea
      privileged among peers

exhale slowly on the outgoing tide
      emptying our inboxed Self

of all trivial thoughts, worries, games
      until our mind floats out quietly

concentrated on the life raft
      of recurring breath.

For a few brief minutes, the tide stands still
      enjoys a calm that cannot last.

It turns, a gathering storm at its back
      whipping other faraway seas

churning up from the chaos of lives
      waves of needs in its briny arms

carries them back to our wrack line
      where we now stand alert, ready,

mind full, inhaling with the tide
      the tattered flotsam of Others

cast into our lives, gasping
      to breathe free again.

BAY WINDOWS

Looking out
at low tide, visions
at your feet
seem endless:

the wrack line
gifting the beach
with teeming remnants,
tidal pools pixilated with
minnows and broken shells,
abandoned whelk homes
with green crab squatters,
burnished sea glass,
glistening jellyfish blobs,
the thousand small depressions
of razor clams and steamers,
sanderling hieroglyphs.

Lift, lift your gaze
past the seagulls
kiting above impotent boats,
focus outward on the shimmer
rising from the hot sand,
follow it out to the horizon
where the sea seems to begin,
feel the wind on your cheek
whispering illusions, allow your eyes
the beyond, what's out there, past where
you want to stop, imagine a dive
beneath calm waves
into Thoreau's *living morgue.*

Part the suffering sea
with your love,
choose to cross it
risking everything.

Beyond

ARS POETICA

A poem should be palpable and mute
As a globed fruit ...
A poem should not mean
But be.
(Archibald MacLeish, Ars Poetica)

Sorry, Archie ...
A poem should be firm
as a tart Granny Smith,
eloquent and bright
as a luscious lemon ...
and there's nothing a poem
should not be and do
including *mean*.

It can wear
the sound of a Bach cantata
the smell of honeysuckle
the taste of sourdough bread
the touch of reunited lovers
or the eyes of the golden eagle

to see across the divide
of money and color,
speak for those muted by birth,
poverty, geography ...
its metaphors be *for*
but also resist, oppose

go beyond a rainbow future,
wrestle to describe
the death of unarmed black men
the starvation of children
in the unjust, turbulent
now.

41

As long as its tongue remains agile
and its mouth full of convictions
may its art be and *mean*
when it needs to sing
the early warning
of the canary
in the dark.

AUGUST VILLANELLE [1]

He never was in prison, not even to visit
all those bars and all that dark
what must they do to the spirit?

You need more than grit
in a place that stark
he never made it to prison, not even to visit.

It's not just the roaches and the shit
you smell — or take — from fists or remarks,
what those can do to the spirit ...

when you're told you can't sit
with a light and read after dark ...
he never knew prison, never even a visit.

From the Bastille to Abu Ghraib, you're spit
upon, reviled, executed by the reigning monarchs
what might that do to his spirit?

Pinochet's too "old," "sick," "decrepit"
they said. Still, as he strolled casually in the park
his mind smelled days with no visits
his cell haunted by Allende's spirit.

TRANSFER STATION [2]

They wear kerchief masks, stinking steam rises
ghostly scavengers sifting ash,
a *gringo* arrival interrupts, surprises.

Stepping slowly, they return to rakes probing trash.
Hungry backs arched, mothers, fathers, children
search for metal, wood, anything to sell for cash.

Mexico City, 1969, land of the PRI, compost garden
of a revolution gone stale
of good intentions diluted, hardened

into slogans, bureaucracies and jails
spawning, among many, Eusebio and Maria
whose toil here cannot afford to fail.

A blackened can is retrieved, a broken bottle of Sangria,
saved: grinding blood work, the kind
their hero fought to prevent. Zapata

himself, were he here today, would climb
these smoking, smelly mounds, strip the tools
from the pickers' hands, wrestle the tines

into pistols, lead the charge against the fools,
greedy betrayers of his life and death.
A child, old enough to be in school

runs proudly, all out of breath
clutching a dead rat. The father, readjusting his hat,
slips the prize into his bag, with practiced stealth.

A rusty Olds, spewing diesel, rolls in, discharges two fat
soldier-cops into the polluted sun,
waving their sub-machine guns at us *gringo* brats.

You must not see this: the Revolution has won
(those imported side arms strongly proclaim).
No one must see this: the Revolution is done.

BAGHDAD POINSETTIA [3]

Tricked by the heat
of scorched earth, it uncoils into life
pushes up scarlet through a concrete ribbon
flanked by patriotic craters

its thirsty roots anchored
in Mesopotamia's sleeping bones
covered now by rivers
of innocent blood

and it screams
at the televised sulfur sky
reflecting the sound and light show
of our newest civilization, waiting,

waiting in vain
for *Guernica*
to be born again
in anger.

EXTRAORDINARY RENDITION [4]

*To **render:** submit, give what is due, surrender, yield, depict, interpret, melt down, reduce, give, make available.*

Down the street from the Green Zone
the bookkeeper renders his altered monthly account
to the Provisional Authority

in Abu Ghraib, a soldier renders
the nightly interrogation report
to his CIA boss

at a military checkpoint, an Iraqi civilian
renders his weapon
to a scared 20-year-old Marine

amidst the rubble, after a roadside bomb
a photographer renders the destruction
for the world to judge

in the remains of a Baghdad kitchen,
in a bombed-out house
a mother, anxious about her missing son,
renders the lamb sauce
until it evaporates
through the open roof
into the deadly air

at the airport, an unmarked Gulfstream Jet
authorized by covert presidential directive
registered in Dedham, Massachusetts
the bluest of States, the cradle of liberty
extraordinarily renders
her son to Egypt
for torture.

THE HIVE [5]

In a small Nevada town
a very young man rises early
from the comfort of bed
and wife, dons a uniform
starched for duty
heads for the office.

Worker bee in his cubicled hive,
the joystick warrior mans a console
patterned after *Grand Theft Auto.*
His flat-screen ripples
with sweet, swaying poppies,
wedding parties, *bad guys.*

Seven thousand miles removed,
the dice have been rolled. A Predator
drone armed with a Hellfire missile,
leaves home, hovers silently,
obliterates the *high-value* target.
Then, he launches another ...

Twelve hours later, laying rubber,
the warrior commutes home, cruises by
the attractive nectar of casino lights
blinking in the distance.

Honey, I'm home!

FOUR BOYS ON A BEACH, JULY 16, 2014 [6]

Black clouds mushroom from the ground in Gaza City.
Fire from the bombs has warmed the cobblestones.
Moments of smoldering quiet are shattered by mourners crying out.

Cooped up for nine days, the Bakr boys escape, to play and cry out.
They have been warned of the beach by their elders in Gaza
but they've only *heard* shells, all they *know* are stones.

When the precision missile explodes on the jetty's crumbling stones
one cousin dies, the other three run, their pain crying out.
Seconds later, they too are splayed on the beach in the City of Gaza.

In the prison of Gaza, soon, *the very stones will cry out.*

OWENSBORO, KY 1936 [7]

The crowd swarmed
buzzing like hornets
twenty thousand strong
making merry well in advance.

Schoolchildren ran free as kites,
tangled in trees and lampposts
to celebrate the hanging,
learn right from wrong.

The gallows' stairs creaked
beneath black, shoeless feet,
a hush blanketed
the hanging party.

The lever snapped,
the trap door clanged
and the rope thumped
its way to tautness.

The children's dawn lesson
was Rainey Bethea,
swinging in the wind,
twenty-two-year-old feet, jerking.

Next day in school, perhaps
one teacher turned from the children,
faced the blackboard, scratched
with crumbling white chalk:

r e v e n g e ?
c
i
t
s
u
j   ?

RAIN, IRAN [8]

Soaked, soggy for weeks,
we complain
again and again.

The rain, deaf
to our inconvenience
spreads its porous umbrella
slakes the thirst of trees,
garden plantings,
decorates leaves
with beads that cling,
then drop
one by one
to irrigate the earth.

Puddles everywhere,
minor dammed irritants,
inflate into imaginary seas
flooding all concerns —
we drown,
we think.

In Tehran,
another rain
whips horizontal,
sniping steel searches
for rebellious hearts, finds
Neda Agha Soltan, age 26,
without violin or fiancée,

rain that reddens
the land frozen
by bearded clerics,
forsaken theology, land
that will thaw again
in time,
with the *green wave*
of her final aria:

I'm burning, I'm burning!

BASTA! [9]

The bullets fly, again —
faster than falcons,
slower than the light
they extinguish randomly,
for six innocents
standing in the way.

Guns don't kill.
Bullets had the privilege
of draining the lifeblood
from Martin, Bobby and John
and the endless succession of victims
that our mythological militia
even after Tucson
continues to justify.

Have we fallen in love with grief
and our teddy-bear shrines,
bagpiped Amazing Grace
and presidential platitudes
pontificating about a better nation
while the NRA owns
most of the pols feigning horror
sending *thoughts and prayers*
attending the funerals,
but unwilling to *represent?*

The bullets will continue
their unobstructed flight,
steel peregrines honing in,
until we finally scream
for the wounded and the dead
to those we've elected:
read, amend, ban
BASTA!

BP and Me [10]

Beyond Petroleum?
You drown all life
in your Deepwater Horizon,

rape the ocean floor
with your twisted, behemoth

phallus, your black sperm spawns
devastation hundreds of miles

from your gushing wellhead,
your prophylactic pipe fails.

Every week,
I thrust your nozzle
into my tank
and pull the trigger.

Eleven workers dead.

Brown pelicans, oil-slicked
endangered wings stilled,

Kemp-Ridley turtles
incinerated by floating fire,

dragonflies glued to reeds,
coral reefs, rainforests of the seas,

slowly dying in the dark,
oyster filters strangled,

all the silent sounds
of petroleum death,

and the black marsh grass
no longer able to sway.

ONE MAN'S FRUIT STAND [11]

Mohamed Bouazizi, without work,
his education on hold
was hawking kumquats, golden
as the sun, and passionately
red persimmons.

That day,
the dictator's inspector came
found him unlicensed, confiscated his scale.
Then, the weight of Mohamed's anger
tipped in favor of Northern Africa.
He showered with petrol, lit the match
that set countries ablaze. Tahrir Square glowed
Lybia, Yemen, Syria ignited
Bahrain and the Emirates bubbled, even
Tel Aviv and London Town simmered.

For two weeks
Mohamed lived with that burning,
visited once by the dictator
dutifully trailing cameras.
One week after
his fire went out,
Tunisia's burned earth
scorched the dictator's heels
all the way to Saudi Arabia.

One man's
fruit
stand.

ORIOLE [12]

Migrant, free-wheeling
passerine, you *are* Baltimore

when you rap your mellow, staccato
song loudly, orange and black

orange *on* black, sporting
those colors long before

the Earl of Baltimore, web sitcoms
and your neglected neighborhood.

I want to believe, have to imagine
that you paused there in a red maple

near Gilmor Homes, locked eyes
with Freddie Gray and, with claws forward

on a dying branch, you took to the air
as he watched you sweep away,

orange and black flashing, minutes before
his spine was severed and his voice box crushed.

And that you, unimpeachable witness,
circled back to that tree

and on its highest live branch, began
to build your finely woven nest, hanging it

precariously, way out on that limb.

GRANT PARK, NOVEMBER 4, 2008 [13]

Where Daley's goons had cracked heads,
fed the earth patriotic blood
under a tear-gas sky,
the trampled grass of hope
awaits with joy the man
out of Africa, out of Illinois.

Tears inch down, reflecting.
A pastor invokes with strength,
blesses with certainty.
A circle of flags,
imprisoning the crowd, agrees.
A diva warbles and whoops
our bursting bombs.

Here's the man!
Out of a motorcade, onto the stage
somber as the night-sky moment
he promises a puppy, and —
only a chance, this time.

Do we need gods so elusive
we have to build them
from our wispy fantasies,
install them on pedestals
of shifting sand?

Is the man asking:
why can't *you* be the ones
you have been waiting for?

ON DJT READING *THE SNAKE* [14]

Older than Adam,
I want to set the record straight —

I am Nuwa, woman-headed
creating the first human, then another,
one at a time. I play, make a third,
then another, enjoy watching
each come to life. Tiring,
I dip a rope in clay, flick it
so blobs become humans
wherever they land.

I am the umbilical cord
joining all humans to Mother Earth.
I am Amduat creating Ra, the Sun
and everything under it.
I am Ouroboros, the sea enclosing the world
tail-eating, proclaiming eternity.
I am Rainbow Snake, water-god
writhing forth creeks, rivers and oceans.

I am Ahi, swallowing the primordial ocean
from whom all creation is released
when Indira splits my stomach
with a lightning bolt. Wiser than Eve,
I am cast as Satan and cursed. Still
I'm unblinking, logical, guard the underworld
carry messages between good and evil.
I don't attack, but I do defend.

I am not the devil immigrant
of your chosen lyrics. I am the cobra
you cannot charm, the python
measuring your girth, the copperhead, coral,
cottonmouth and sidewinder coiled, waiting.
I am the *narrow fellow in the grass*
who disappears you know not where.
I will be your worst nightmare in the Rose Garden.

LITURGY AT FORT HILL (*CAPE COD NATIONAL SEASHORE*)

                                                    Let us petition

for the drop of dew on a blade of grass that reflects the morning sky

for the meadow grass that conceals the returning lark's nest

for the lark that whistles a dark victory from its yellow breast, watches

for the fox on the hunt, that carves its own trail, kits in tow

for the egret, that stands at attention, feet wet, at the passing of the fox

for the hawk, drifting, that lasers the air for movements in the marsh

for the heavy air, still breathable, that inhabits the sky

for the night sky that displays its blackboard of stars

for the stars whose light still races, unobserved

for all the tomorrows of whatever exploded in the beginning.

NEXT

Heaven   or hell
limbo   or Limbaugh,
what awaits
in pleasure   or torture
for   ever?

Sitting   on clouds
dampening   our behinds
butchering   the harp
chorusing   Amazing Grace
contemplating   divinity? ...

or planted   in hell,
feet   (and every other
body part)   to the fire,
pitchforking   embers
on our neighbors
for a barbecued   eternity?

Have some males   not been told
that the 72 virgins who await
will only date   eunuchs ... ?
that   at some point
in a few trillion years
those satanic caretakers
are bound   to doze off
and hellfire   flame out forever ... ?

Are we still
waiting   for messiahs
while passively   lasering
on our innards?   or
do we really want   to return
step down   a notch,
don animal suits   and fly
or gallop   or roar?

Released   from gravity
why not   fly free
dive   into space
whiz   through cosmic dust
that stings   our spirit,
bungee-jump
from the Pluto   dwarf
to the volcanoes   of Io
to the blue   Pleiades,
feast on wonder ...

as our earthly   plastic bodies
melt   at hypersonic speeds
our backpacked baggage   shreds
streamlined into   compressed ideas
and passions,   a whirlpool
of creativity   swirling into
white-hot holes   of extinction
where   some lucky atoms
might survive   gather   re-arrange
for the next   *big bang* ... ?

Notes

1. Augusto Pinochet, Chilean dictator, overthrew Salvador Allende in a U.S.-backed coup on 9/11/1973 and ruled until 1990. In 1998, on a visit to London, he was arrested for crimes against humanity and installed by the British government in comfortable exile on the luxurious estate of Wentworth in Surrey.

2. Incident witnessed by the author in the spring of 1969 of dump-pickers in one of the slums encircling Mexico City.

3. U.S. carpet-bombing of Baghdad: 12/17/1998–12/20/1998. Clinton impeachment hearings: 12/19/1998.

4. Based on the case of Hassan Mustafa Osama Nasr, kidnapped by the CIA in Milan on 2/17/2003 and rendered to Egypt.

5. USAF base in Indian Springs, Nevada, thirty-five miles northwest of Las Vegas, used for remotely-controlled drone bombings of Iraq and Afghanistan.

6. Incident in Gaza, Palestine when the boys, playing on the beach, were fired upon and killed by an Israeli gunboat.

7. The hanging took place at 5:32 a.m. on 8/14/1936. Rainey Bethea's victim was 70-year-old Lischia Edwards. This was the last public execution in the U.S.

8. June 2009 was a rain-soaked month on Cape Cod. Neda, philosophy student and musician, was shot dead in Tehran while returning to her car after protesting the election of Ahmadinejad on 6/20.

9. "Gabby" Giffords, U.S. Congresswoman from Arizona, was shot in the head on 1/8/2011 while campaigning, but survived. Eighteen others were shot; six died. She is now an advocate for stricter gun regulations.

10. BP oil spill, largest marine petroleum disaster in history, began on 4/20/2010 and lasted until 9/19/2010. An estimated 210 million gallons were released into the fragile Gulf of Mexico environment.

11. Mohamed, street vendor in Sidi Bouzid, Tunisia, self-immolated by fire on 12/17/2010 in protest and died three weeks later. His action ignited the Arab Spring movement.

12. Freddie Gray, 25-year-old black man, was arrested by Baltimore police on 4/12/2015 and, according to eyewitnesses, beaten and transported unsecured in a police van to a hospital. He died a week later of injuries to his spinal cord. The medical examiner ruled his death a homicide. Six police officers were charged with lesser crimes and all were acquitted after bench trials.

13. Election night speech of Barack Obama in Chicago. Forty years earlier, Grant Park had been the scene of Mayor Daley's violent crackdown on demonstrators. Last two lines borrowed from Alice Walker's *We Are the Ones We Have Been Waiting For: Inner Light in a Time of Darkness* (New Press, 2006).

14. Music by Oscar Brown, 1963; lyrics by Al Wilson, 1968; misused by DJT several times since.

Reviews

"There is something deeply satisfying about a poet with depth and range. Leo Thibault is such a poet. Microscopically, he examines ordinary experiences with tender appreciation—an elderly friend's smile after visiting his 'missus' in a nursing home, a father gently kissing his sleeping son so as not to wake him, and a knife probing an oyster shell 'for the life-and-death spot / in the hinged entrance.' All these mundane moments build 'the wondrous architecture and truth of a quiet life.' Then, as Thibault shifts, with surgical skill, into the haunting last section, *Beyond*, he exposes the dark underbelly of our species—its complicity with cruelty. Poetry, Thibault declares in 'Ars Poetica,' 'should be firm / as a tart Granny Smith.' Additionally, it 'needs to sing / the early warning / of the canary / in the dark.' Each and every poem in *Bay Windows* does both. Dare to read this poetry collection from beginning to end, and over again."

-Alice Kociemba, author of *Bourne Bridge*

"As an anchor of sorts for 'our lives out of balance' (from the poem 'Koyaanisqatsi'), this poet carefully regards the surface of things, particularly the on-going comfort of dailiness in [his] immediate surroundings. This poet is very much a citizen of the world. From the personal and local to international events, [his] aim is to determine truth and focus anger at injustice, while always returning to the connections that bring us together. I think readers of this manuscript will recognize and find consolation in this effort at wholeness."

-Cleopatra Mathis, author of *What to Tip the Boatman?* and *White Sea*

"I admire the poems in Leo Thibault's *Bay Windows* for their keen and tactile description, and their accuracy, and the way the poems unfold with suspense and surprise, like presents. But what I revere most in them is their truthfulness. I feel here is a guide, a steady voice I can trust, follow as he explores the Cape and the world. Truth is always liberating, but in our time, jaded, and numbing; in which words have been devalued, it seems to have become a pleasure as well. It's a joy to listen with him as our steps crunch on the winter beach, to lift our heads to the night sky with its 'blackboard of stars.'"

-Keith Althaus, author of *Ladder of Hours* and *Rival Heavens*

With Gratitude

Writing is a solitary occupation, but revising, at its best, is a communal undertaking. Most of these poems were refined and sculpted into their final shape with the help of my current and former fellow Narrow Land poets: Lucile Burt, Donna O'Connell-Gilmore, Dianne Ashley, Ginia Pati, Chuck Madansky, Susan Graesser, Wilderness Sarchild, Paula Erickson, Marjorie Block, and Beeby Pearson, who died last year. Also, my "Wise Living" writer/friends Lee Tupman and Jon Holt. To Angela Howes, editor, thank you for your always cheerful kindness and patience. In addition, much gratitude is extended to all the established poets whose workshops over the years have polished my writing, especially Cape Cod poets Keith Althaus, whose insights were always too modestly offered, and Lorna Blake, for her extensive historical knowledge and teaching skills. Finally, heartfelt thanks to Kaimi Rose Lum of Snow Library for her shared love of poetry. All helped me "say the most with the least."

About the Author

Leo Thibault was born and raised in Greenville, New Hampshire, before moving to Cape Cod in 1974. He started writing seriously after his retirement from the Forestry Camp in Brewster in 1999. For a decade, Thibault was a member of the Salt Wind Poets, a writing group that was featured annually at First Night Chatham. Since then, he has belonged to the Narrow Land Poets, a working group which began in Wellfleet, Massachusetts, and meets monthly. Over the years, he has attended workshops conducted by Galway Kinnell, Carolyn Forche, Martin Espada, Derek Walcott, Robert Pinsky, and others, including every Dodge International Poetry Festival from 1996 until 2010. His most recent awards have been at the 2016 Jacaranda Poetry Festival and the New Port Richey Art Festival in Florida, and the Veterans for Peace contest in Centerville, Massachusetts. His work has appeared in *Prime Time*, *The Cape Codder*, and *The Aurorean*. This is his first published collection.